Santiago de Compostela

EVEREST

Text: Xosé Carro Otero

Photographs: Imagen MAS, Miguel Raurich
and Archivo Everest

Editorial coordination: Francisco Bargiela

Diagrams: José Manuel Núñez

Cover Design: Alfredo Anievas

Digital image processing: Marcos R. Méndez

Translation: EURO:TEXT

Carretera León-La Coruña, km 5 – LEÓN
ISBN: 84-241-3626-8
National Book Catalogue Number: LE. 366-1998
Printed in Spain

EDITORIAL EVERGRÁFICAS, S. L.
Carretera León-La Coruña, km 5
LEÓN (Spain)

James and his brother John, out fishing with their father Zebedee, are summoned by Christ to become apostles. Polychrome alabaster carving on a small altarpiece of English origin (15th century). Santiago Cathedral Museum.

THE ORIGINS OF SANTIAGO

The history of **Santiago de Compostela** is to be traced back to the dawning of the 9th century, to the discovery of the tomb of St James the Apostle at a site around which the town we know today was to gradually take shape and flourish. Such a circumstance as this inevitably leads us to ponder how St James —born in Palestine, son of Zebedee and Mary Salome, brother of John— ever came to be buried here in Galicia. In order to find the answer to this question, there are three considerations that we must bear in mind:

1) The Biography of the Apostle

St James *the Greater* became a disciple of Jesus at the same time as Peter, Andrew and his own brother John.

2) His Relation with Spain

It is well-known by all that upon the death of the Saviour, the Apostles, following Christ's instructions, ventured out to the four corners of the world as it was known then in order to teach the Gospel. According to tradition, St James came to the Iberian Peninsula, (in those times called *Hispania*), where the memory of his preaching still endures at several places, such as Viana do Castelo, Braga, Padrón, Lérida and Cartagena. On the outskirts of the town of Caesaraugusta (the present-day Zaragoza, Saragossa), James was visited by the Blessed Virgin Mary, who came miraculously to comfort him from Palestine, where she still lived, leaving him as a reminder of her presence a column or *pillar,* which is kept at the Basilica in Zaragoza. On his return to Jerusalem, James was apprehended and beheaded. Thereupon his disciples devoutly gathered up his body and, setting off from the port of Jaffa (the present-day Haifa), headed for **Iria Flavia** in Hispania (a coastal town that once stood near what today is the village of Padrón in Galicia), on a journey that took them across the Mediterranean, along the Strait of Gibraltar and around the coast of the Iberian Peninsula. From Iria the disciples then carried the body inland on a cart drawn by oxen which, as legend will have it, was given to them by a woman by the name of Lupa. Finally, they laid the saint's remains to rest in a funerary structure built at a place called *Libredón,* situated near a *castro* (or prehistoric fortified settlement) whose existence and location is still remembered today by one of the streets in Santiago's old quarter, namely *Calle del Castro.* Once they had brought James' body to these lands, the saint's disciples set off once more on their evangelizing mission from the very tomb in which he had been buried. Two of them, Theodore and Athanasius, who in all likelihood stayed behind to serve as the first guardians of this *apostolic site,* would in time also be buried in this tomb, one on either side of their *master.*

Panoramic view of the old quarter of Santiago de Compostela from Monte Pedroso, the hill situated to the north-west of the town.

Translation of St James' body across the sea from the Palestinian port of Jaffa to Iria Flavia in Galicia. Polychrome alabaster carving on a small altarpiece of English origin (15th century). Santiago Cathedral Museum.

3) The Discovery of the Tomb

With the passing of the centuries and the ever-changing fortunes they brought, the tomb of St James was to gradually fall into oblivion. Amongst the many specific reasons why this should happen were the various persecutions to which Rome subjected the early Christians, an oppression that was felt to a greater or lesser extent in all corners of the Empire; the Barbarian invasion of Galicia in the early 5th century; and the subsequent Moslem overrunning of the region in the early 8th century. Little by little, the small funerary structure was destroyed as a result of its exposure to the elements and its ruins came to be hidden by plant cover. Indeed, the only indication that remained as to its existence was the vague memory that the local inhabitants passed on, by word of mouth, from generation to generation, namely that somewhere in *Gallaecia* (Galicia), at a place called *Libredón,* lay the relics of St James *the Greater,* Christ's Apostle.

In the early 9th century, a hermit by the name of Pelagius, who lived in a church dedicated to St Felix which itself was situated at *Libredón,* is said to have perceived, on successive nights, a series of inexplicable lights and sounds that seemed to emanate from the wood that lay nearby. Aware as he was —as were so many others— that this very spot was the one that allegedly concealed the tomb of St James, Pelagius hastily set off for the neighbouring town of Iria Flavia, 20 kilometres away, where Theodomir, the bishop of the local diocese resided, in order to inform him of such strange happenings, which he himself believed to be miraculous signs indicating the exact location of the tomb.

Thereupon, the prelate visited the site accompanied by his entourage. Trees were felled, undergrowth cleared, unearthing a small building that lay in ruins and which comprised two levels: an upper one featuring a small altar, and a lower level or crypt in which three burials were discovered.

The latter were immediately attributed to the Apostle himself (the central tomb), and to his two disciples, Theodore and Athanasius (those on either side).
On receiving the glad tidings, the King of Asturias Alfonso II *the Chaste,* accompanied by his noblemen, hurried here from Oviedo in order to admire the Apostle's sepulchre. The king ordered a small *basilica* to be erected over the site of the tomb, whereby the original altar belonging to the latter was retained.
At the same time, he arranged for the foundation, on adjacent lands, of a monastery. Here, a community of twelve Benedictine monks from Oviedo led by Abbot Ildefredo were entrusted with the task of providing for and supervising the incipient veneration of the relics of St James the Apostle.
Thus the town of Compostela was born, its first buildings being the said *basilica* and *monastery.*
Its name was believed, up to a few decades ago, to have derived from the Latin *Campus Stellae* (Field of Stars), in memory of the miraculous lights that revealed the location of the tomb. In recent years, however, a number of other explanations for the name have come to challenge this theory.
In 1955, the excavations carried out beneath the Cathedral unearthed the tombstone belonging to Bishop Theodomir of Iria, the man who according to tradition was responsible for the discovery of St James' tomb. The finding of this tombstone has greatly reinforced the authenticity of the traditional account, both as a result of the fact that Theodomir had expressly wished to be buried near the body of the Apostle and not in Iria, his episcopal see, and because the date of his death, recorded by the inscription appearing on the tombstone as being 847, is in keeping with the general chronology that has been assigned to the great event he played such an important part in.

12th-century miniature portraying the discovery of the tomb of St James the Apostle, in the early 9th century, by Bishop Theodomir of Iria Flavia. From the book entitled "Tumbo A" which contains several ancient documents. Santiago Cathedral.

BUS:XPI

THE PILGRIMAGE TO SANTIAGO

The tradition of the pilgrimage to Santiago de Compostela, established by the countless pilgrims that ever since the discovery of the Apostle's tomb in the early decades of the 9th century have flocked here uninterruptedly to worship the mortal remains of St James the Greater *(orationis causa)*, was to be one of the factors conditioning the development of the town of Santiago and the key to the great prestige it enjoys on the *Old Continent*. The pilgrimage is often referred to in Spanish as *La Peregrinación Jacobea*, the adjective *jacobea* deriving from the

View out over the rooftops of the south-eastern part of the old quarter of Santiago de Compostela from the "Torre de la Carraca", one of the towers of the Obradoiro Façade.

name Jacobo, a variant of Santiago. Although in purely quantitative terms the pilgrimage has undergone great ups and downs over the more than a thousand years it has existed, it can be said that the afflux of pilgrims was relatively speaking at its height between the 11th and the 15th centuries. The popularity of the pilgrimage waned somewhat from the 16th to the late 19th centuries, but has risen again in the course of the 20th century, soaring spectacularly on the occasion of the last *Holy Year* in 1993.

Anyone who undertook the pilgrimage to Santiago did so under extremely harsh conditions, taking into account its geographical position right at the very edge of the European continent (indeed it has been said that it was preferable to *go five times to Rome than just once to Santiago)*. Consequently the pilgrims would try to join up with others on their way —the bigger the group the better— in order to be able to provide mutual aid and protection in face of the many perils awaiting them on such a long journey.

The Santiago Cathedral chapter provided aid for those pilgrims who could prove they were in real need, giving them enough money to help them find their way home and new clothes if their own ones were worn out. The changing of clothes took place at a stone basin near the basilica. On the roof one can see a stone *Agnus Dei* (Lamb of God, the lamb symbolizing Christ) that features, embedded in its back, a large bronze cross. Both the lamb and the cross are Romanesque elements belonging to the 12th century, the cross being known as Cruz dos Farrapos in Galician or Cruz de Harapos in Spanish, in reference to the ragged clothes that were left next to it.

On completing their sacred journey, the pilgrims would buy two objects as proof of the feat they had achieved. Firstly, there was the *concha de vieira* or scallop shell, which they sewed onto the brims of their hats and other parts of their attire and baggage. Secondly, they purchased a document called the *Compostela* which, issued by the Santiago chapter, served as confirmation of their having achieved the status of pilgrim.

◀ *Portrayal of "St James, Christ's Soldier" (St James the Moor-slayer). Having been the guardian of the Christian forces during the Reconquest, the Apostle became the Patron Saint of Spain. "Tumbo B", Santiago Cathedral Archive.*

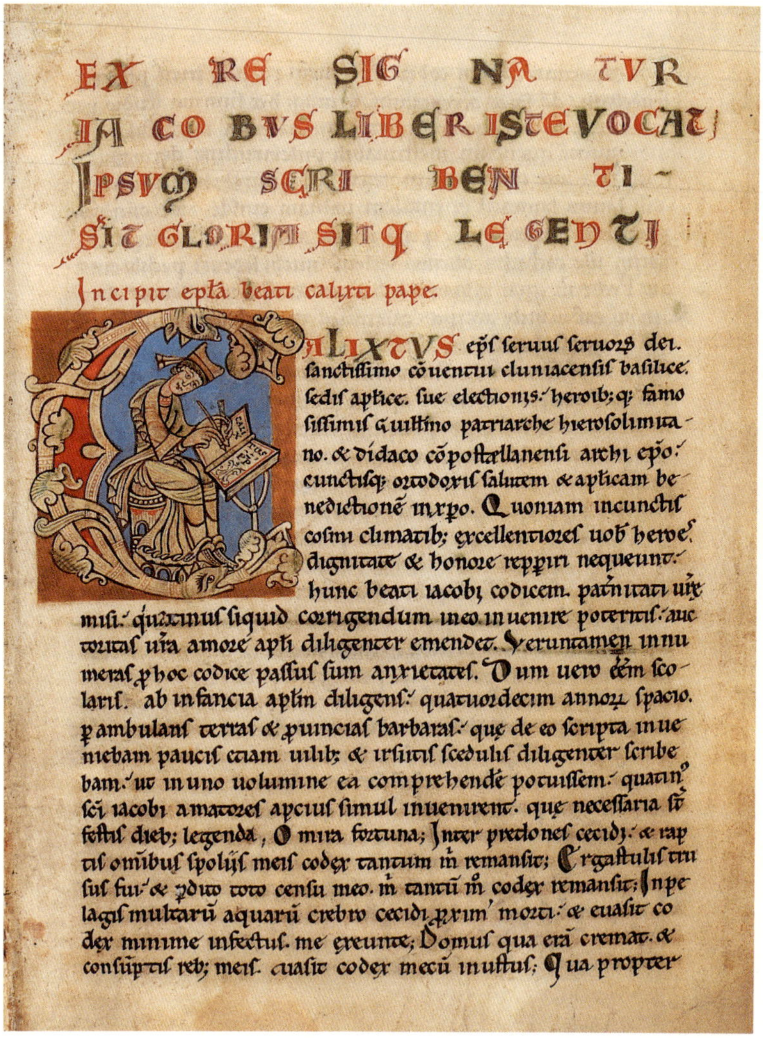

The first page of the «Codex Calixtinus», the important manuscript dating from the mid 12th century that includes the first known description of the Pilgrim's Route to Santiago and the town of Santiago de Compostela. Santiago Cathedral Archive.

St James the Apostle depicted in pilgrim's attire. 18th-century sculpture by Gambino on display at the Cathedral chapterhouse. ►

THE PILGRIMS' ROUTE TO SANTIAGO

Having taken the decision to undertake the pilgrimage to the tomb of St James, the unending stream of pilgrims would start their journey from the very doors of their own houses, making up their exact itinerary as they went on, in accordance with the various alternatives afforded them by the *road network* existing in Europe at the time. It can be said, therefore, that the generic term *Pilgrims' Route to Santiago* refers not to a single route but rather to a combination of possible itineraries featuring a myriad of points of departure —the pilgrims' own dwellings— and a common destination, namely the Apostle's sepulchre. Indeed, the only justification for the use of this term lies in the very fact that those who made their way to Compostela did so by means of the said network. Those who journeyed along the Route with the intention of reaching Santiago were what we can call spiritual travellers, or even *sacred wayfarers.* Taking the above into account and in light of the wealth of cultural developments and exchanges that have taken place under the influence of the Route, in 1987 UNESCO effectively recognized this generic concept of the Pilgrims' Route to Santiago, declaring the latter to be a *Primary European Cultural Itinerary.*

The pilgrimage to Santiago was to receive a great impulse when, in around 1119, it was granted the so-called *Jubilee* or *Holy Year* Privilege by Pope Callistus II. A Holy Year, according to this particular privilege, is any year in which the feast day commemorating the martyrdom of St James —held on the 25th July— falls on a Sunday, which happens to occur every 6, 5, 6 and 11 years. Those pilgrims who in a Holy Year completed the journey to the basilica in Santiago were able to benefit from the concession of a *full indulgence* and obtain many other spiritual rewards.

Plan of Santiago dating from the mid 18th century. Watercolour owned by the Institute of Galician Studies.

Preceding two-page spread, the cathedral's western façade, also known as the Obradoiro (featuring, on the right, the Cloister; and, on the left, the Archbishop's Palace).

SANTIAGO DE COMPOSTELA: AN HISTORICAL-ARTISTIC DESCRIPTION

The **historical and monumental centre** of Santiago de Compostela, which in former times was surrounded by a defensive wall, originally emerged over an oval-shaped area whose main axis, running from north to south, measured a little over 700 metres. Over the last one thousand years, the evolution of this Old Town has witnessed the gradual incorporation of a succession of both architectural styles and trends in urban development, in a process uninterrupted by either natural or human catastrophe. From an artistic point of view, this would explain why vestiges of the Pre-Romanesque are seen to exist alongside magnificent manifestations of the Romanesque itself and other examples of, amongst other styles, the Gothic, the Plateresque, the Baroque and the Neoclassical.

There are three characteristic features of Santiago that should be highlighted here. Firstly, owing to the fact that the said historical and monumental centre lies on a hillock, many of its streets were laid out on a slope, as a result of which, in order to construct the major squares and buildings of the area, a series of land terracings and levellings were required. Secondly, one is struck by the aesthetic contrast of, on the one hand, its narrow streets, many of which date from the Middle Ages and bear names reminiscent of the former guilds and the trades that were carried on in each one (such as Calle Calderería —Cauldron Makers' Street, Calle Azabachería— Jet Workers' Street, etc.) and, on the other, the expansive Baroque squares, above all those surrounding the Basilica or Cathedral. Lastly, it should be noted that the most widely used construction material, both for buildings and for surfaces, is granite, a stone which, so abundant in this region, has been crafted into ashlars or slabs by expert stonemasons.

A TOUR AROUND THE TOWN

Plaza del Obradoiro: This rectangular square is the largest in Santiago and is flanked by four buildings: the *Cathedral,* the *Hostal de los Reyes Católicos, Rajoy Palace* and the *University Vice-Chancellor's Offices.*

Right, aerial view of the cathedral and the buildings and squares surrounding it.

Centre, the cathedral's Obradoiro façade.

Below, the old cathedral photographed from its north-western section.

The Cathedral. The vast area of this square devoted to the cathedral building is in fact made up of three easily distinguishable parts, namely a central section and two side ones.

The central section is none other than the main cathedal façade, which bears the same name as the square itself, *El Obradoiro.* Built in Baroque style in the first half of the 18th century by architect Fernando de Casas y Novoa, this façade came to replace a formerly existing one and features elements to be assigned to various epochs. Thus, the flight of steps giving access to the cathedral was erected in the 17th century and leads to what is erroneously referred to as the *Old Cathedral* but which in reality is a 12th-century vaulted Romanesque-style edifice, one which forms the true foundations of the Cathedral at this point. Soaring up to the left and right of the observer are the towers called Torre de la Carraca (*carraca* is the name given to a wooden instrument played during the Easter celebrations) and Torre de las Campanas (or Bell Tower), respectively. Standing around 70 metres tall, the towers feature a 12th-century (Romanesque-style) first level disguised by more recent additions, to which the two remaining levels were added in the 17th and 18th centuries (Baroque style).

The highlights of the rich ornamentation gracing this façade are, from top to bottom, the *effigy of St James the Apostle* (depicted in pilgrim's attire) and, underneath the latter, a star-spangled chest symbolizing the saint's tomb, on either side of which stand the images of St James' favourite disciples, Theodore and Athanasius.

The part of the cathedral lying to the right of the Obradoiro façade belongs to the **cloister,** itself built in the 16th century in Plateresque style and featuring an impressive gallery on its upper level and a strange tower with a tiered roof reminiscent of a dovecote at the southwestern corner of the building.
If we enter the cathedral through the doorway we find on street level at this point of the square, we come into what is the most important sector of the **Cathedral Museum** (the others being the above mentioned *Old Cathedral* and Gelmírez Palace, along with the *Chapel of San Fernando,* itself situated within the cathedral), one which comprises four different storeys. The first two house a variety of archaeological remains, whereas the third storey is on a level with the open section of the cloister, a quadrilateral structure of considerable dimensions (44 m x 44 m) that was used as a burial place for the cathedral canons. Transferred to the cloister some years ago were the basin belonging to a 12th-century Romanesque fountain that had previously stood on the northern side of the cathedral exterior *(the Azabachería façade)* and the two bells that since the 18th century had struck every hour and quarter of an hour at the cathedral *clock tower* (and which, having split, were recently replaced by similar bells). Also to be seen on this level are the *library* and the *chapterhouse,* the former being the place where the renowned *botafumeiro* or censer is kept, whereas the latter features a collection of 16th-century tapestries depicting scenes from the lives of Scipio and Hannibal.
The fourth storey is almost entirely devoted to a further collection of tapestries dating from the 16th to 18th centuries, amongst which there are twelve that were crafted from drawings by Goya at the Real Fábrica de Santa Bárbara in Madrid.

One of the rooms of the Cathedral Museum.

View of the cloister and the tower called "Torre del Tesoro". ▶

Chapterhouse library. Hanging from a stand in the background is the famous "Botafumeiro" (the enormous censer unique to Santiago).

The chapterhouse walls are draped with priceless 17th and 18th-century tapestries.

The part of the cathedral complex lying to the left of the Obradoiro façade as we face it belongs to the **Archbishops' Palace** *(Palacio de los Arzobispos)*, a building that stretches out beyond the square itself into the adjacent *Calle de San Francisco.* Featuring as it does elements erected in a variety of periods, above all the 16th, 17th and 19th centuries, the oldest part of this edifice, dating from the 12th-13th centuries and only to be seen from the inside, is the one popularly referred to as **Palacio de Gelmírez,** itself a remarkable example of secular Romanesque architecture (the most noteworthy of the various buildings that go to make up the palace is what was possibly the former dining hall, its vaulted ceilling resting on a series on ribs whose weight is supported by brackets or corbels decorated with several scenes). The so-called *Arco de Palacio* is an archway or passage which, having been opened up right at the heart of this oldest part of the Archbishops' Palace, connects Plaza del Obradoiro with that other famous square, Plaza de Azabachería. The passage features a flight of steps that serves to overcome the difference in level between the two squares and was erected about forty years ago to replace the earth slope that had previously made it possible for horses and carriages to pass this way.

Room of noble design (possibly a former dining hall) at Gelmírez Palace.

Façade of the Hostal de los Reyes Católicos.

Hostal de los Reyes Católicos. Since 1953 a luxury hotel belonging to the chain of Spanish paradores or state-run hotels, this building had up to that point in time been the Gran Hospital de los Reyes Católicos, the 'hospital' or hospice founded by the Spanish monarchs in the late 15th century in order to provide accommodation and care for the pilgrims that arrived in the town. The area lying just in front of the building, marked off by a series of pillars and chains, is where in former times one could enjoy the *right of asylum* (no criminal taking refuge here could be apprehended by the law without the prior permission of the person in charge of the Hospital). The beautiful Plateresque façade, the work of architect and sculptor Enrique de Egas, is literally overflowing with sculpted figures (depicting Apostles, saints curing illnesses, etc.) and is flanked on either side by contemporary 16th-century Spanish coats of arms.

The balconies and windows underwent Baroque-style alterations in the 18th century.

◀ *Patio de San Juan, one of the four courtyards at the Hostal de los Reyes Católicos bearing the names of the Evangelists (in this case, St John).*

The layout of the building's interior is seen to revolve around four interconnected arcaded courtyards The two courtyards lying adjacent to the entrance, between which stands the former hospital *chapel* (itself featuring an interesting grille and a transept with spectacular ornamented pilasters and a graceful lantern), were built in the first decade of the 16th century. Erected in a Plateresque style, they in fact constitute what was the original building and have at their centres fountains dating from the time of their construction. The other two courtyards were built as a result of extension work carried out on the building in the 18th century and are therefore Baroque in style. Lying at the centre of each is a small church-shaped structure standing over an artesian well.
Visitors not staying at the hotel can have a guided tour of the building on its ground level, including the said courtyards.

The Hostal de los Reyes Católicos takes up the entire northern side of Plaza del Obradoiro.

Palacio de Rajoy. Built on the orders of Archbishop Rajoy in the second half of the 18th century, this palace was devoted to a number of purposes. Thus, it was a *confessors' seminary,* that is, a residence for those priests who heard confessions at the Cathedral, many of whom were referred to as *lenguajeros* owing to the fact that they spoke several European languages in order to attend to foreign pilgrims. At the same time, it provided accommodation for the members of the cathedral chapel, namely the music master, choirboys, etc., and also served as the local town hall and even as its prison. Nowadays, apart from still being the home to Santiago Town Council, the building houses some of the departments of the Galician Autonomous Regional Government or Xunta, along with the Council for Galician Culture (Consello da Cultura Galega).

Built in Neoclassical style according to the plans drawn up by the engineer of French origin Charles Lemaur, the structure of the palace is arranged into five sections, the central one of which, graced by a series of sturdy columns, is surmounted by a pediment featuring a sculpted portrayal of the miraculous apparition of St James the Apostle at the legendary Battle of Clavijo. This scene is likewise depicted by the equestrian statue of St James the Moor-slayer that crowns the pediment. The finishing touch to the end sections is provided by segmentally curved pediments emblazoned with the coat of arms of the founder bishop.

From a small terrace on the northern side of the palace, the one nearest to the Hostal de los Reyes Católicos, one can see the mid 18th-century Baroque **Church of Las Angustias de Abajo.** (A similarly-named church, *Iglesia de las Angustias de Arriba,* is to be found in northeastern Santiago). The church façade, crowned by a series of statues depicting the cardinal virtues, has a central section featuring a superimposed arrangement including the Spanish coat of arms, a scene of the *Souls of Purgatory* and an image of the Blessed Virgin of the Sorrows holding Christ on her lap after He had been taken down from the Cross. To be seen inside the church are outstanding 18th-century polychrome wood sculptures belonging to the school of Felipe de Castro.

Façade of Rajoy Palace, the edifice lining Plaza del Obradoiro on its western side.

Rectorado de la Universidad. (The University Vice-Chancellor's Office). Built in the mid 17th century to house one of the University's colleges, namely the Colegio Menor de San Jerónimo. This is a structure of modest appearance whose outstanding feature is the 15th-century Neo-Romanesque portal that constitutes the only element to have been saved of the Old Hospital (also called St James) that was demolished in the 17th century. The interior boasts a small, simple cloister where an inscription dating from 1652 informs us that in that year the Colegio de San Jerónimo, founded by Archbishop Alonso de Fonseca y Acebedo, was transferred here.

Portal of the Colegio de San Jerónimo, the building gracing the southern side of Plaza del Obradoiro.

View of Plaza de la Azabachería and the Monastery of San Martín Pinario, featuring the church of the latter, as seen from the cathedral rooftop.

PLAZA DE LA AZABACHERÍA

Moving on from the Plaza del Obradoiro, we reach this square by means of the above mentioned passage, the **Arco de Palacio.** Plaza de la Azabachería is so called in memory of the guild of jet-craftsmen or azabacheros, whose workshops once lined both the square itself and the adjoining street of the same name. Objects crafted from jet (a black-coloured lignite) were and still are very typical of Compostela, above all items of jewellery in which the stone —either plain or carved— is set in precious metal. Many shops in Santiago specialize in offering a wide range of craftsman-made silver and jet jewellery, which they sell at very reasonable prices.

Plaza de la Azabachería is flanked by three extraordinary buildings: the **Cathedral,** whose northern façade gives onto the square; the **Archbishop's Palace;** and the Monastery of **San Martín Pinario.**

The **Northern Façade of the Cathedral,** also known as **the Azabachería façade,** was built in the second half of the 18th century in a style marking the transition from the Baroque to the Neoclassical. It replaced the former 12th-century Romanesque structure, which we know was adorned with a large number of magnificent sculptures. The most outstanding features of the present-day façade, apart from the coats of arms and medallions that grace it, are the *statue portraying Faith* attributed to the artist Gambino and, crowning the whole, the sculpture of St James the Apostle, who is depicted with two praying kings at his feet.

From the said narrow little street, Calle de la Azabachería, one can see a small belfry which, although embedded in the cathedral wall, belongs to the **Church of La Corticela,** an originally free-standing Romanesque building that in the course of the 17th century would be embraced by the cathedral fabric.

The building known as **San Martín Pinario** was a Benedictine monastery from the time of its foundation in the 9th century until the advent of ecclesiastical disentailment in 1836 that forced members of religious orders to abandon their cloisters. At a later date the edifice was reconverted to house the Council Seminary of the Santiago de Compostela Archdiocese, a function that it still serves today.

For the last few decades, San Martín Pinario has also been home to the Theological Institute, the Galician School of Social Studies and a University Hall of Residence.

Spreading out as it does over an area of 20,000 square metres, the present-day building was erected in Baroque style from the 17th to the 18th century, thus replacing the former structure that stood on this site.

Northern façade of the cathedral, also known as the Azabachería façade.
On the right one can make out part of the Archbishop's Palace.

Monastery of San Martín Pinario. Main doorway crowned by the Spanish coat of arms and a statue portraying the saint to whom the monastery is dedicated, St Martin of Tours.

Giving onto the Plaza de la Azabachería is the main façade, at the centre of which a flight of steps leads up to the entrance doorway. Above the latter, arranged on successive levels, we can observe a *statue of St Benedict,* an impressive balcony, the coat of *arms of Spain* and the façade's crowning glory, a group sculpture depicting *St Martin of Tours,* the monastery's patron, cutting up his cloak in order to dress a poor man.

The interior of San Martín Pinario, part of which is open to visitors, boasts a superb **processional cloister** with a fountain at its centre, the work of architect Casas y Novoa. The building's own church, the dimensions of which surpass even those of many cathedrals and whose façade gives onto another square, namely Plaza de San Martín, is the regular venue, along with the eastern section of the complex, for important exhibitions and other cultural events.

As we look out from the San Martín Pinario steps, our eyes are greeted by an interesting view of the Cathedral, one which comprises the two towers of the Obradoiro façade, the lantern featuring tall slim windows and a dome rising up over the crossing (the point at which the two vessels forming the Latin cross ground plan of the cathedral intersect), and the Clock Tower, the tallest of all the cathedral's vertical members. On looking closely, between the said lantern and the Clock Tower one can discern a small pillar crowned by an Agnus Dei (the Lamb, a symbol of Christ) that bears on its back a bronze cross, the so-called **Cruz dos Farrapos** that we mentioned earlier in the section entitled *The Pilgrimage to Santiago.*

Standing at right angles to the northern façade of the cathedral is a group of buildings that form part of the **Archbishop's Palace** or *Palacio Arzobispal.* What we have before us here is basically a series of modifications and additions which, carried out in the 19th century, are of no particular artistic merit.

Two-page spread overleaf, Plaza de la Quintana. In the background, the steps leading to Casa de la Parra. On the right of the square, the Monastery of Antealtares.

Casa de la Parra (House of the Vine), so-called on account of the intertwining vine branches adorning its balcony.

PLAZA DE LA QUINTANA

This square is reached along a winding lane, *Tránsito de la Quintana,* that skirts the cathedral from Plaza de la Azabachería. Also known as *Plaza de los Literarios* in memory of the batallion formed by university students to help ward off the French in the Spanish War of Independence (1808), Plaza de la Quintana is arranged into two levels connected by an extremely wide flight of steps. The upper section is called Quintana de Vivos *(Quintana of the Living)* and the lower one Quintana de Muertos *(Quintana of the Dead),* owing to the fact that the latter was the town cemetery right up until the late 18th century. Lining the square on each of its sides are the following monumental structures:

Casa de la Parra. This small Baroque-style palace, dating from the 17th century, features a flat roof, a continuous balcony supported by corbels, along with a doorway and windows decorated with motifs in the form of bunches of fruit. Up on its roof we see a large chimney typical of those fashioned in its day, finishing as it does in a kind of turret adorned with a false or blind balustrade.

Monasterio de Antealtares. This monastery ranks as the second oldest building in Santiago, having been founded immediately after the discovery of the remains of St James the Apostle, at a time when work was already underway on the basilica that Alfonso II the Chaste had ordered to be built over the saint's tomb. Ever since its foundation, the monastery has belonged to the Benedictine Order, its building having served its original purpose right up to the present day, except that is for a short period in the late 15th century, during which time its community of monks joined that of the nearby monastery of San Martín Pinario, their place being taken by a community of nuns.

Partial view of the Monastery of Antealtares, as seen from Plaza de la Quintana.

Church of the Monastery of Antealtares. High altar.

The impressive wall of granite facing us as we contemplate the building —broken only by a series of simple, regularly spaced latticework windows— dates from the last restoration work that was carried out on the monastery in the late 17th and early 18th centuries.
A memorial stone reminds us of the above-mentioned *Batallón Literario,* the battallion of university students who were presented with their standard at a solemn ceremony held in this very square. To be found in the narrow street running between Casa de la Parra and Antealtares, the so-called Vía Sacra or Holy Way, is the modest façade marking the entrance to the **monastery church.** Visitors to the latter are inevitably struck by the beauty of its magnificent Baroque retables, whilst awaiting them in the choir is an 18th-century period organ which, having recently been perfectly restored, is used in the Baroque music concerts that are held in the church. Once inside the church one can visit the interesting **Museum of Sacred Art** belonging to the monastery and at the same time get to know some of the interior buildings that go to make up the monastic complex.

Outer portal that leads through to the Puerta Santa or Holy Door, which can be seen through the grille.

Canónica. This arcaded building owes its name to the fact that in former times it was the institutional residence of the cathedral canons. This would also explain why it is divided up into several independent living quarters. Built in Baroque style in the 18th century, it replaced an earlier structure which, serving the same purpose, had stood on this site since the early 12th century.
Eastern façade of the Cathedral, also known as the **Quintana façade.** Constructed in Baroque style in the second half of the 17th century, in an attempt to give a more uniform appearance to the east end of the cathedral, which aesthetically speaking had suffered as a consequence of the many alterations carried out on this part of the building between the 12th and the 17th century.
On contemplating this façade, the attention of the observer is drawn by its two magnificent portals. The one situated nearest the flight of steps leading up from the square is closed off by an iron grille and is adorned by 27 sculptures. Commanding the doorway at the top are the images of the Apostle and his disciples Athanasius and Theodore, flanked by 24 figures that originally graced the Romanesque choir that up until the early 17th century formed part of the cathedral. This doorway leads through to a small courtyard, at the far side of which stands the world-renowned **Puerta Santa** or Holy Door, which is only ever opened during the Holy Years. The door is opened amidst great ceremony on the 31st December of the year before and is subsequently closed with similar pomp and circumstance on the last day of the Holy Year.
The other portal, lying adjacent to the clock tower, is known as the **Puerta Real** or Royal Door, owing to the remarkable Spanish coat of arms presiding it.

View of the cathedral from the north-eastern corner of Plaza de la Quintana, featuring the Holy Door and the Clock Tower.

PLAZA DE LAS PLATERÍAS

Plaza de las Platerías (Silversmiths' Square) is lined on two of its sides by the Cathedral and is flanked on the other two by the Chapterhouse and the Bank of Spain, the latter dating from the middle of this century.

At the centre of the lower level of the square stands a fountain, **Fuente de los Caballos.** Rising up above the fountain horses is an allegory of the town of Santiago in the form of the image of a woman resting on the Apostle's tomb while holding, in her right hand, the star that had signalled the spot where the saint's remains lay.

From this square we can enjoy views of two parts of the Cathedral, namely the **Southern façade** —also known as **Platerías façade**— and a section belonging to the cloister.

The former lies on the upper level of the square and is adjoined on its right-hand side by the **Clock Tower,** which is also referred to as *Torre de la Trinidad* and *Torre de Berenguela.* What we have before us here is the oldest façade of the cathedral, since this was where work on the original Romanesque cathedral began in 1075.

The lower level of the façade features two portals whose tympana provide a portrayal of scenes from the Life of Christ. Thus, the left-hand tympanum depicts *The Temptations of Christ in the Desert* and an image of the *Penance of Mary Magdalene,* whereas the right-hand one shows *The Capture of Christ on the Mount of Olives, Simon of Cyrene Carrying the Cross, Flagellation, The Crown of Thorns* and *The Adoration of the Magi.*

Above the tympana is a series of sculptures, many of which were brought here from the Northern façade when the latter was replaced, as we have pointed out earlier, in the 18th century. Standing at the centre of this group, above a representation of Abraham, is an image of Christ in Majesty, to the right of which we see a statue of St James himself. Also to be seen here are *The Expulsion of Adam and Eve from Paradise,* some signs of the Zodiac (Sagittarius and Pisces), along with the herald angels announcing the Last Judgment.

The upper level of the façade features two windows framed by multifoil arches, the structure as a whole being crowned by a 17th-century Baroque balustrade similar to the ones culminating most of the cathedral walls. Behind the latter is a triangular pediment at whose apex we find an *Agnus Dei,* the Lamb of God, complete with a cross on its back.

Plaza de las Platerías (Silversmiths' Square) flanked by the shops —located on the lower level of the cathedral cloister— that have given it its name.

One of the two Romanesque portals —the western one— that give access to the cathedral from Plaza de las Platerías.

Giving onto this square is the eastern side of the cathedral **cloister,** the fabric of which leaves no doubt as to the fact that it is to be attributed to the early 16th-century Plateresque. Further up the cloister wall are several ornamental elements, such as the Spanish coat of arms and the images of *St James at the Battle of Clavijo, The Translation of the Apostle's Body from Palestine to Galicia* and *The Tomb with the Star.* Crowning the wall is beautiful openwork cresting and, at the point where this section of the cloister merges into the cathedral façade, there is a small corner projection resting on a gigantic stone shell that evidences great architectural expertise.

Casa del Cabildo. Constructed in Baroque style in the 18th century, the chapterhouse building was conceived as a way of providing an ornamental front for the southern side of the square (its depth is minimal). Such a purpose is reflected by an inscription in Latin that can be read on the lintel of the second floor central window.

Fuente de los Caballos (Fountain of Horses) and the so-called "Chapterhouse".

THE CATHEDRAL INTERIOR

As we enter Santiago Cathedral we become aware of the original structure of the edifice, the exterior of which has undergone many alterations and has been extensively added to in the course of time. The original cathedral church, built from 1075 to 1188 in pure Romanesque style, has a Latin cross ground plan. **Capilla Mayor** or High Chapel. Lying at the centre of the top arm of the Latin cross, the High Chapel was covered in gilt wood and ornamental stones during the Baroque, in the second half of the 17th century. The **high altar,** lined with sheets of engraved silver (dating from the late 17th-early 18th centuries), is presided over, as is its side grillework, by a 13th-century Gothic polychrome stone sculpture of *St James the Apostle*. St James is depicted here in a seated posture in typical pilgrim's attire with a tunic and short cape; in his left hand he holds a long stick or pilgrim's staff, from which hangs a gourd for carrying water. Higher up above this silver ensemble is another statue of St James, on this occasion in polychrome wood and in a standing posture, but likewise dressed in pilgrim's clothing. Flanking this statue are the images of two kings who are portrayed on their knees in prayer.

View of the nave running along the main arm of the cathedral. At the back, the high chapel.

The Crypt, commanded by the chest containing the remains of St James and his disciples Theodore and Athanasius.

◀ *The High Chapel, whose silver altar is situated directly above the crypt where the Apostle's body lies.*

Covering the whole of the high chapel is a solid, sumptuous gilt wood baldachin or canopy supported by a series of massive angels. The canopy bears the Spanish royal coat of arms and yet another representation of the Apostle, this time on horseback, portrayed just as he is said to have appeared at the Battle of Clavijo, sowing terror amongst the Moslem forces, an image known as St James the Moor-slayer. The chapel enclosure, which also features choir stalls carved by the artist Francisco del Río in the middle of the present century, is illuminated by three great lamps, the central one of which is Louis XV-style, whereas the two side ones are Italian, the work of Roman artist Balladier.

Built into the pilasters marking the entrance to the high chapel is a pair of 16th-century Plateresque bronze *pulpits* crafted by Juan Bautista Celma. Appearing outside the pulpits are a pair of alms boxes, each of which is flanked by a polychrome stone sculpture depicting, respectively, St James the Less (son of Alphaeus), the first bishop of Jerusalem and St Mary Salome, the mother of the Apostle.

The famous "Botafumeiro" censer as it swings to and fro along the cathedral transept, kept in motion by the eight «tiraboleiros» who pull at one end of the rope.

The head «tiraboleiro» ties the "Botafumeiro" to the rope from which it is hung.

Rising high up above the cathedral crossing (the point at which the two arms of the Latin cross intersect), where a few years ago a new altar facing the public was erected in compliance with the recommendations of the II Vatican Council, is the lantern or dome. Featuring as it does a series of windows and vaults that are clearly Gothic in style, the lantern was built in the 14th century as a replacement for a previous Romanesque structure. A curious mechanical device to be seen in the cathedral is the one that rests on the four large pilasters of the crossing. From it hangs a rope with an artichoke-shaped silver end. This, of course, is the machine that makes it possible for the famous *botafumeiro* (a censer standing approximately 1.6 m tall and weighing 60 kg) to *fly* through the cathedral. Unique to Santiago Cathedral, the botafumeiro is used only in major liturgical celebrations, either to pefume a relic with incense as it is brought out to take part in a procession or as a thanksgiving ceremony upon the termination of Mass. Once it has been attached to the said rope in place of the silver artichoke, a single man sets the botafumeiro swinging, whereupon a further eight, the so-called *tiraboleiros*, by rhythmically pulling at the other end of the rope, make it sway back and forth from one side of the transept to the other, flying so high that it almost touches the vaults.

Affixed to the southwestern pilaster of the crossing is a Romanesque bronze column that houses the walking staff used by St Francis of Sena on his pilgrimage to Compostela in the 13th century.

Before leaving the crossing, one should note that both of the church limbs, that is, both the larger and the shorter arm of the Latin cross, are divided into three vessels separated by means of a series of rectangular pillars embedded with columns. The nave is the tallest of the said vessels and is covered with semicylindrical barrel vaulting, whereas the aisles flanking it are lower in height and feature ribbed vaults. Above the aisles is a gallery or triforium that opens out onto the nave through a series of twin or paired windows. Another noteworthy feature of the cathedral is that both the aisles and the gallery above them are so arranged that visitors can walk right around the church perimeter, a fact which makes it possible to hold processions inside the cathedral and moreover greatly eases the flow of the masses of pilgrims who flock here.

The little chamber situated behind the sculpture of the Apostle that presides the high altar. The chamber is reached through the ambulatory. ▶

The ambulatory, at the back of which, flanked by two Romanesque sculptures, one can see the Holy Door, which is only ever opened during Holy Years.

Ambulatory. This is the aisle or passage that encircles the high chapel. As we walk around the ambulatory from the right-hand side, we notice on our left two little doorways giving access to stairways. The first of these leads down to the crypt where the tomb of the Apostle lies, whilst the second takes us up to the *camarín* or little chamber where one can embrace the statue of St James that presides the high altar.
In the **crypt,** which was remodelled in the late 19th century and extended a few decades ago, the visitor to the cathedral can contemplate what remains of the tomb of the Apostle and his disciples. This is the very tomb that was discovered by Bishop Theodomir of Iria at the beginning of the 9th century and above which lay the altars of the three successive basilicas that were built between the 9th and the 11th/12th centuries in order to afford protection for the said sepulchre. Through a doorway opened up at the centre of one of the walls of the tomb, which is quadrilateral in plan, one can see an excavated chapel on whose altar rests the so-called *urna del Apóstol* or Apostle's Urn. The latter is a silver chest fashioned by local craftsmen in 1886 in what is a mixture of Palaeo-Christian and Romanesque styles and contains the mortal remains of St James the Apostle and his disciples Theodore and Athanasius, which had originally been buried in three separate graves in the floor of the said tomb.
Situated up above the high altar, the little chamber referred to as the **camarín** affords anyone who so wishes the chance to kiss the image of St James, for many centuries a tradition amongst pilgrims, who

thus provided a fitting climax to their pilgrimage. Hanging from the centre of the chamber ceiling is a small silver lamp that was presented to the cathedral in order to illuminate this section by Gonzalo Fernández de Córdoba, the great captain who led the forces of the Catholic Monarchs to victory during the famous Italian campaign. The lamp is a reminder of the captain's visit to the cathedral in 1512. Halfway up to the chamber, there is an entrance to the retrochoir, which is also visible from the ambulatory through the stained glass windows. Worthy of our attention here is a small 17th-century Baroque retable featuring scenes from the Life of St James. Also of interest is the rather unsophisticated "chest" that was opened up in the middle of the floor as a secret hiding place for the remains of the Apostle and his disciples when it was feared that the English troops under Francis Drake (that at one point were laying siege to the town of A Coruña) might reach Santiago and desecrate the sacred tomb.

Capilla de Mondragón. ▶

Capilla del Pilar.

Back down in the ambulatory, we come across seven chapels and the *Puerta Santa* or Holy Door that open out into the outward-facing wall.

Capilla del Pilar is a 18th-century Baroque chapel founded by Archbishop Monroy, whose tomb complete with praying statue and epitaph is the highlight of the wall on the Epistle side. The chapel altar is dedicated to Our Lady of the Pillar (Virgen del Pilar), the Blessed Virgin Mary having appeared to St James when he was preaching the Gospel at Caesaraugusta, the present-day Zaragoza. Richly and profusely decorated with elements and motifs relating to the tradition of St James, this chapel features a series of stars and shells, together with the so-called Cross of St James, itself an allusion to the sword brandished by St James when he miraculously appeared as a warring knight at the Battle of Clavijo.

Capilla de Mondragón. A 16th-century Plateresque addition to the cathedral, this chapel was founded by the Mondragón family, whose coat of arms embellishes the grillework closing off the entrance. Crafted from polychrome terra-cotta, the chapel retable portrays the complete scene of the *Descent from the Cross* (the work of Corniellis of Holland).

Capilla de San Pedro (St Peter's Chapel). This is one of the original five Romanesque chapels that graced the ambulatory. Its design is that which was shared by all but one of the said chapels, featuring, amongst other elements, a semicircular ground plan, a quadrispherical shell-shaped vault and three openings. It also has an 18th-century Baroque retable and the tomb, complete with recumbent statue, of Doña Mencia de Andrade, a lady from Compostela who lived in the 16th century.

Puerta Santa or Holy Door. Having already briefly mentioned this doorway above on referring to Plaza de la Quintana, we should also point out that it was constructed in the early 16th century, following the example of the Basilica in Rome, whose own Holy Door had been opened up in the late 15th century. In what is a symbolic tradition, it is through this doorway that pilgrims enter the cathedral in Holy Years, a fact that we are reminded of by the inscription that can be read on the parchments held by the two Romanesque figures flanking the door. These figures originally stood in the former cathedral choir, which was dismantled in the early 17th century. The inscription reads: *People come from all over the world to proclaim your glory, Lord.*

MARQUESES DE
JUAN ARMADA Y
MARIA DEL ROSARIO

Capilla del Salvador.

Capilla del Espíritu Santo. Old tombs and a mural painting portraying "The Descent from the Cross".

Capilla del Salvador. *(Saviour Chapel).* Also known as the *Chapel of the King of France,* due to the fact that King Charles V the Wise donated it a considerable amount of money in the 14th century. Lying at the centre of the ambulatory, this chapel is Romanesque in design, but unlike the others has a quadrilateral ground plan and features two side niches at its back wall. Appearing on the capitals gracing the arch at the chapel entrance are inscriptions alluding to King Alfonso VI and Diego Peláez, Bishop of Santiago, both of whom lived at the time this part of the cathedral was built (the late 11th century). Awaiting us inside the chapel are a 16th-century Plateresque retable and two notable tombs, namely that of the former *regidor* or mayor of Santiago Francisco Treviño, embedded in the left-hand wall, and the one belonging to canon Antonio Páramo y Somoza, who died in 1786 as bishop-elect of Lugo. In former times, this was where the pilgrims to Santiago would collect their *compostela,* the certificate presented to them by the cathedral chapter in recognition of their having completed the pilgrimage. On displaying this document, any pilgrim who did not have sufficient means to pay his own way was afforded free accommodation and food for three days at the Hospital de los Reyes Católicos. Nowadays this custom is maintained by the Hostal de los Reyes Católicos, which offers free breakfast, lunch and evening meal to the first ten pilgrims to arrive each day.

Capilla de Nuestra Señora la Blanca. A 13th-century Gothic addition, this chapel has an unremarkable modern neo-Gothic altar and several tombs belonging to its founders, the España family, whose coat of arms presides the entrance doorway.

Capilla de San Juan Apóstol *(St John the Apostle Chapel).* Standing in symmetry to that of San Pedro, Capilla de San Juan was built at the same time as the latter and therefore ranks as another of the five original Romanesque chapels. The chapel underwent extension in the 16th century, the cost of which was the loss of its central section. It features a Baroque altar with the image of the martyr St Susan, who shares with St James the Apostle the distinction of being the patron saint of Santiago de Compostela.

Capilla de San Bartolomé *(St Bartholomew's Chapel).* Likewise Romanesque in style, the distinguishing feature of this chapel is its pentagonal ground plan. Its simple 14th-century Plateresque altar stands in stark

Capilla de la Corticela.

contrast to the magnificent tomb that is embedded in the left wall and which, fashioned in the same style and period, houses the remains of the canon who had achieved the dignity of *maestrescuela,* Diego de Castilla, the great grandson of King Peter the Cruel (the tomb sculpture, crafted from Coimbra stone, a limestone, is the work of master Arnau).

Having at this point come to the end of the ambulatory, we now turn into the northern arm of the transept, the one which, leading to the Azabachería façade, contains the following chapels:

Capilla de la Concepción *(Chapel of the Immaculate Conception).* As is revealed by the ornamentation of one of its entrance doorways, this chapel is 16th-century Plateresque. It features two altars that are separated by a door and whose outstanding elements are the image of Our Lady of the Immaculate Conception and an 18th-century Baroque group sculpture representing the Descent from the Cross. Situated in the Epistle wall is the tomb of canon Antonio Rodríguez, sculpted by Corniellis of Holland in the first half of the 16th century.

Capilla del Espíritu Santo or **Capilla de la Soledad** *(Chapel of the Holy Ghost or Chapel of Solitude).* Access is gained to this chapel at the point where one of the seven Romanesque "lesser doorways" to the cathedral once stood. The chapel itself was erected in Gothic style in the 13th century, although it would later undergo certain alterations. The retable, dedicated to Our Lady of Solitude, was transferred here in 1944 from the retro-choir (the back wall of the choir), having up to then been located under the organs in the main arm or nave. It was made of wood in the early 17th century in order to replace a Romanesque stone retable, some of whose statues we have mentioned as having been re-used in various parts of the cathedral. One of the seven interesting tombs —two of which are very old and feature recumbent statues and low Gothic arcosolia—, the one belonging to Archbishop Alonso Sánchez de Moscoso, has at the back of the niche that houses it the only old mural painting to be seen in the cathedral: a 15th-century Descent from the Cross.

At a point once occupied by another of the original Romanesque chapels, the semicircular structure of which is still clearly noticeable, a stepped passageway was opened up in the 17th century so as to provide a connection between the cathedral and the **Church of Santa María de la Corticela,** a 12th-century Romanesque structure that had previously been an independent building (We mentioned this church earlier on describing the Plaza de la Azabachería). Standing at the end of the passageway is the church portal, whose tympanum includes an image of the *Adoration of the Magi.* The interior distribution of the church is one featuring a nave and two aisles (with wooden ceilings), in addition to three apses. On the right-hand wall as one enters the church lies the tomb which, dating from the first half of the 14th century, belongs to Gonzalo Eans, a canon who was to attain the dignity of cardinal.

Polychrome wood group sculpture depicting St James "the Moor-slayer".

Capilla del Cristo de Burgos.

Opening out from the left-hand wall of the passageway leading to the former Church of Santa María de la Corticela is the 17th-century **Capilla de San Andrés** *(St Andrew's Chapel),* featuring an early 18th-century retable. Our Lady of Luján, the patron saint of Argentina, has been worshipped here since 1947. On either side of the steps belonging to the northern façade called the Fachada de la Azabachería lie the chapels of San Antonio (to the right) and Santa Catalina (to the left). Whilst their 18th-century Baroque retables are of no great interest, it should be pointed out that the walls separating the chapels from the said staircase contain the tombs —complete with recumbent statues— of Prior Juan Vidal (late 16th century) and the bishop of Orense, Alonso I (15th century).

In a small room adjoining the chapel of Santa Catalina, the figure of St James the Warrior *(the Moor-slayer)* is worshipped, as portrayed by an 18th-century polychrome wood processional group sculpture.

As we continue on our way around the cathedral nave, we come across the following:

Capilla de la Comunión *(Chapel of Communion).* This is the part of the cathedral in which the Blessed Sacrament is venerated. Dating from the 18th century and having a circular ground plan, this chapel boasts, in addition to its Rococo retable, the sepulchres of archbishops Lope de Mendoza and Bartolomé Rajoy. The former archbishop was responsible for the founding, right here, of the chapel that preceded the present-day structure, which was in turn commissioned by the latter. The sculpted armorial bearings belonging to each of the said bishops appear on the lintels of the two doors leading into the chapel.

Capilla del Santo Cristo de Burgos. This chapel was founded in the second half of the 17th century by Archbishop Pedro Carrillo y Acuña, who, being as he was from Burgos, dedicated it to the famous Santo Cristo or Blessed Christ, an image so devoutly venerated in his home town, a replica of which is seen to preside the mid-18th century main altar. The presbytery walls hold the tombs and praying statues pertaining to archbishops Carrillo and García Cuesta. The latter, having lived in the second half of the 19th century, also became a cardinal of the Roman Catholic Church. The most outstanding architectural feature of the chapel is its Neoclassical portal.

Next we come to two doorways, the first of which —decorated in a Baroque-Plateresque style— leads the visitor down to the so-called *Old Cathedral* (see section above on the Obradoiro façade). The second doorway takes us up to the gallery or triforium.

Pórtico de la Gloria *(Doorway of Glory).* Regarded as a veritable masterpiece of Romanesque sculpture, this doorway was built by Master Mateo in the period spanning the years 1166 and 1188. Having been designed to serve as a porticoed entrance to the cathedral, it comprises three arches, a central one and two side ones that correspond to the cathedral nave and aisles. Dominating the central arch tympanum is the figure of Christ surrounded by the four Evangelists, each of whom can be identified by means of their respective symbols, namely the eagle (St John), the writing desk (St Matthew), the bull (St Luke) and the lion (St Mark). Appearing on either side of the latter is a group of figures in prayer representing the "people of God", beneath which there are eight angels carrying the instruments of the Passion. The tympanum is framed by an archivolt representing the 24 elders —depicted here playing a series of musical instruments— mentioned by St John in the Book of the Apocalypse. Supporting the tympanum at its centre is a mullion in the form of a cluster of columns, the top of which is graced by a sedentary or seated image of St James the Apostle, whilst its base features a portrayal of the Tree of Jesse, that is, Christ's human and divine ancestry. Turning our attention to the columns on either side of the central arch, we will notice, on the right, a series of sculptures depicting St Peter (holding some keys), St Paul, St James, St John (whose symbolic eagle appears at his feet), and on the left, the figures of Moses (with the tables of the Law), Isaiah, Daniel (here young and smiling) and Jeremiah.

Without doubt the most noteworthy of the two side arches is the right-hand one, its tympanum featuring at its centre the heads of Our Lord the Father and the Son. Two groups of figures, one on either side of the latter, are seen to represent Heaven —angels lovingly carrying the blessed in the folds of their robes— and Hell —horrible demons torturing the wretched damned.

There are two further points of interest regarding the Pórtico de la Gloria. Firstly, evidence exists supporting the view that its sculpted ensemble was in fact polychrome; and secondly, standing with its back to the Pórtico and leaning against the mullion, there is a statue representing none other than the artist responsible for the Doorway, Master Mateo. The latter is commonly known in Galician as *santo dos croques* or the *saint of the knocks,* owing to the fact that in ancient times the people of Santiago would bring their children here and knock their heads against the stone crafted by such an outstanding artist, in the hope that, by the magic of touch, the sheer intelligence and genius of Mateo would rub off on their offspring.

Image of St James the Apostle.

Pórtico de la Gloria or Doorway of Glory.

Central column (mullion) of the Doorway, adorned with a sculpture of St James the Apostle.

Upper section (tympanum) of the central arch of the Doorway of Glory.

Sculptures portraying the apostles Peter, Paul, James the Lesser and John gracing the right-hand pilaster of the central arch (as we face it) of the Doorway of Glory.

Arch on the right-hand side of the Doorway of Glory affording a view through into the aisle that lies behind it. ▶

Statue depicting, in a praying posture, the artist responsible for the Doorway of Glory, namely Master Mateo (a statue nicknamed "the saint of the knocks").

As we leave the Pórtico by its right-hand side arch, we come across another pair of doorways arranged symmetrically to those lying opposite that we have described above.

Capilla de las Reliquias *(Chapel of the Relics).* This chapel is preceded by a vestibule or antechamber —which it shares with the *Chapel of San Fernando*—, the far wall of which contains the tombstone belonging to Bishop Theodomir of Iria, the discoverer of St James's tomb in the 9th century. The Chapel of the Relics can only be seen by looking through the windows in its doorway.

The chapel altar, built subsequent to the 1921 fire that destroyed the previous one dating from the 17th century, was fashioned from cedarwood in Neogothic style and houses a large number of reliquaries, some of which are true gems of the art of working precious metals. The most important of these reliquaries dates from the 14th century and contains the head of St James the Less, son of Alphaeus and first bishop of Jerusalem, crusaders having brought the relic here from the holy city two centuries earlier. Moreover, the chapel also boasts the tombs, complete with recumbent statues, of several royal figures, namely: Ferdinand II and Alfonso IX of León; Doña Berenguela, queen of Alfonso VII the Emperor; Doña Juana de Castro, queen of Pedro I of Castile; Count Raymond of Burgundy, who was married to Doña Urraca of Castile; and Pedro Froylaz, the count of Traba, who was the guardian and tutor of Alfonso VII.

Capilla de San Fernando. Nowadays this chapel is one of the rooms that goes to make up the Cathedral Museum, and as such holds a number of important, valuable exhibits. Amongst these are the processional monstrance crafted in Plateresque style by Juan de Arfe in the mid-16th century; the lavishly adorned early-18th century Baroque lunula commissioned by Archbishop Monroy in gold and gemstones; the early-19th century Imperial style chalice and cruet set in gold and diamonds, a gift from Archbishop Múzquiz; along with a number of trays, Eucharist dishes, medallions (including one of St Christopher embellished with coral) and ornaments.

Having thus completed our tour of the cathedral nave, and before we move on to the southern arm of the transept (the one facing Plaza de las Platerías), we should stop awhile to appreciate the fronts of the two organs that stand opposite each other across the nave. Being of early 18th-century Baroque style, the latter were paid for by the above-mentioned Archbishop Monroy, a great benefactor, both of the cathedral, the town and the diocese.

The Sacristy. The cathedral sacristy is reached by means of an ante-sacristy which in turn is entered through a 16th-century Plateresque doorway. Even though it is generally speaking of little artistic

Front of the cathedral's northern organ.

Left, the first Plateresque-style processional monstrance to be crafted in Spain.

interest and in quite bad repair, this part of the cathedral, which is closed to visitors, has some paintings from the 18th and 19th centuries.

The Cloister. The next doorway on, belonging to the same style and time, is the one leading to the cloister. At present it is closed to the public, since the cloister enclosure constitutes a sector of the Cathedral Museum, the entrance to which is situated on Plaza del Obradoiro.

A TOUR OF THE TOWN

A stroll around the well-preserved historical centre of Santiago is a truly unforgettable experience, both as a result of the beauty of the various sights to be beheld at each turn and the sheer variety of the latter, all of which form part of what is a *living city*.

Leaving *Plaza del Obradoiro* along *Calle del Franco* —a street renowned for the great number of typical bars and restaurants that line it, affording the visitor the chance to taste the traditional wines and seafood of Galicia— we eventually come out into *Plazuela de Fonseca,* a small square graced by the 16th-century Plateresque building of the former *Colegio Mayor* de Fonseca, the first of the halls of residence to be specifically built to serve the University of Santiago de Compostela, the latter having been founded in 1495 (1995 saw the celebration of its fifth centenary). Under the patronage of Archbishop Alonso de Fonseca, the building remained a hall of residence right up until the mid-19th century, when the Faculties of Medicine and Pharmacy were established here. Nowadays it is home to the *University General Library.* Visitors have free access to the beautiful cloister to be found inside.

Restaurant window in Santiago de Compostela displaying some of the renowned culinary products of the region.

Plazuela de Fonseca. On the left, the façade and tower of the building erected to serve as the hall of residence called Colegio Mayor Fonseca. ▶

A XÉNESE
GALLAECIA FVLGET
A XÉNESE
LIBRE

MODAS

Plaza del Toral, featuring a fountain and the Palace of the Marquises of Bendaña.

We continue our tour along the *Travesía del Franco,* which in turn leads us into **Rúa del Villar,** the most important street in the old town of Santiago, comprising as it does a series of notable houses, most of which are arcaded. This street takes us on to *Plaza del Toral,* the northern flank of which is lined by the 18th-century Baroque palace belonging to the Marquises of Bendaña. Crowning the palace façade is a statue of the mythological figure Atlas, who is depicted bearing the universe on his shoulders.
On leaving Plaza del Toral we set off down **Rúa Nueva,** one of the most outstanding features of which being the 18th-century Baroque *Palace of the Count of Ramiranes,* erected on the site previously occupied by the *Colegio de San Patricio* or St Patrick's College, an institution that was devoted to the education of Irish noblemen. Further along the road we come to the Church of Santa María Salomé, a 12th-century Romanesque structure that has undergone several subsequent additions and alterations. Its porticoed façade boasts a Romanesque image of the Blessed Virgin with the Child, at the centre of the arch, and a 15th-century Gothic group sculpture representing the Annunciation.
At this point, Calle de *Tras Salomé* leads us on into **Calle las Huérfanas,** a street that owes its name to the College founded in the late 16th century by Archbishop Juan de Sanclemente in order to take in the town's orphaned maidens (Sp.: huérfanas = orphan girls). Dedicated to Our Lady of the Remedies, the college was rebuilt in the early 18th century by Archbishop Monroy. It has its own church, the façade of which is to be seen at the left end of the complex, as we face it.

◀ *Traditional shop located on the arcaded street called Rúa del Villar.*

Plaza de Mazarelos, at the heart of which stands the statue commemorating Montero Ríos.
In the background, the building whose construction was funded by Archbishop Yermo.

Plaza de la Universidad. Façade of the School of the Society of Jesus, today the Faculty of Geography and History. ▶

Setting off again along *Calle Cardenal Payá,* we reach **Plaza de Mazarelos,** a square that in times gone by was replete with shops selling meat. Another feature of the square is the *Puerta de Mazarelos,* the only surviving gate of the seven that once formed part of the town walls. Looking through the gate, we can see the *Convent of the Mercedarias Descalzas* (Discalced Mercedarians), which was built beyond the town walls on the orders of Archbishop Girón in the second half of the 17th century. Displaying an early Baroque style, the convent façade features a beautiful group sculpture portraying the Annunciation. Other noteworthy elements of the square are the large building that nowadays houses the Faculty of Journalism (a mid-18th century Baroque structure commissioned by Archbishop Yermo Santibáñez in order to serve as a Jesuit-run House of Exercises) and the memorial statue of José Montero Ríos, the illustrious late 19th-early 20th century jurist and politician who was born here in Santiago. Still standing in the adjacent **Plaza de la Universidad** is the former *School of the Society of Jesus,* along with the church that belonged to it. Having originally been erected in the second half of the 16th century, both were to be reconstructed in Baroque style in the 18th century and subsequently undergo Neoclassical alterations in the 19th. At present the school building houses the Faculty of History and Geography, whereas the church, which has recently been restored, is used as a venue for cultural events of a singular nature.

FACULTADE
DE

Next, our walk around the streets of Santiago takes us down **Calle del Castro,** graced by a statue of King Alfonso II (a gift from the town of Oviedo), and out into what is one of the most interesting parts of town, namely the **Plaza del Mercado** or Market Square, which lies between the *Church of San Félix* and that of *San Agustín.* The origin of the Church of San Félix is to be traced back to the *hermitage of Pelagius,* the man who in the early 9th century saw the luminous signs revealing the location of the Apostle's tomb. The Church of San Agustín, a mid-17th century Churrigueresque structure, belongs to a monastery of the same name which, originally run by Augustinian friars, was later taken over by the Jesuits. Architecturally speaking, the market building itself dates from the middle of the present century and was erected over a section of the old town walls. Consequently, from certain points of the market one can enjoy an interesting view from what amount to be genuine *miradores* or look-out posts. Among the elements encompassed by the view are: **Calle de la Virgen de la Cerca,** a street running concentrically to the said wall; the 19th-century Neoclassical Colegio de la Enseñanza, a school for young ladies commissioned by Archbishop Múzquiz; and, rising up in the distance, on a hillock reached by means of the narrow, steeply climbing **Calle de las Trompas,** the *Convent of Belvís.* The latter institution was founded in the early 14th century by Doña Teresa González. Having been completely rebuilt in the 18th century, nothing remains today of its original fabric. Nevertheless, the convent has a chapel erected in honour of Our Lady of the Portal, who is greatly worshipped by the people of Santiago.

Calle de las Casas Reales (the two buildings pictured here are 15th-century Gothic and 18th-century Baroque, respectively).

Church of San Agustín. One of its towers was never completed.

Spiral staircase at the Monastery of Santo Domingo de Bonaval.

Leaving Plaza del Mercado behind us, our tour takes us on around the **Plazuela de San Agustín,** the square lying at the feet of the church of the same name. Next, we carry on along **Rúa Traviesa,** where we find the late-18th century Baroque *Church of Nuestra Señora del Camino,* and finally come out into **Rúa de Casas Reales.** Outstanding features of the latter are the early-19th century Neoclassical *Church of Las Ánimas,* whose nine remarkable altars portray the Passion of Christ, and a series of Gothic (15th-century) and Baroque houses. Walking on up this street, we come to **Plaza de Cervantes,** formerly known as *Bread Square* owing to the fact that it once contained a number of shops selling both bread and other agricultural products. Standing on one side of the square is the *Church of San Benito* which, founded in the 12th century, was totally reconstructed in the course of the 18th. Inside the church is a beautiful Gothic doorway tympanum depicting the Adoration of the Magi. Leaving Plaza de Cervantes by Calle de la Azabachería, the street once lined with jet-craftsmen's workshops, we then turn into **Calle de la Troya** (second on the right), where we come across a building bearing the same name. This is Casa de la Troya, a former students' inn that provides the setting for the famous novel by Alejandro Pérez Lugín entitled *La Casa de la Troya.* Published in 1915 and belonging to the Spanish literary genre dealing with local customs, *costumbrismo,* the story constitutes a true and very pleasant reflection —penned in a highly romantic key— of the way of life of university students in Santiago in the late 19th century. Such was the success of the novel that to date over a hundred authorized editions have been printed, along with as many illegal ones. Moreover, it has been turned into a theatre play and adpated on several occasions for the cinema. For the last few years *Casa de la Troya* has been open to the public as a kind of museum, a reminder of its own past and the circumstances that surrounded it.

Church façade of the Monastery of San Martín Pinario, along with the flight of steps leading down to its entrance.

Calle de la Troya leads us on to an area comprising two small squares, namely those of San Martín and San Miguel. The most striking feature of Plazuela de San Martín, the larger of the two squares, is the Church of San Martín Pinario which, dating from the first half of the 17th century, forms part of the monastery of the same name. Its Plateresque façade, preceded by a curious flight of steps that leads down to the church entrance, has the appearance of an altar retable. Commanding its upper section is an image of St Martin, who is seen offering half of his cloak to a poor man; further down the façade is a series of tidily arranged statues of saints, whilst at its base lies the emblem of the Valladolid Benedictine Congregation, to which the Monastery of San Martín Pinario belonged. The highlight of the vast church interior —arranged as it is on a Latin cross ground plan— is the splendid 18th-century Baroque retable gracing the high altar, behind which lies a no less magnificent choir whose stalls were crafted in wood by sculptor Mateo de Prado in the first half of the 18th century.

From the highest point of the adjacent Plazuela de San Miguel, where one can see the church dedicated to Michael the Archangel —a church that existed as far back as the 12th century but whose present-day building dates from the 19th century— our itinerary now continues along **Calle de Algalia de Arriba,** on the left of which we find the *Museo de las Peregrinaciones,* a monographical museum focussing on the history and the art surrounding the pilgrimages undertaken to the tomb of St James the Apostle.

Following the road around to the left, we come out into **Calle de San Roque,** a street that takes its name from the chapel and hospital founded here in the 15th century in order to invoke the protection of St Roque against epidemic diseases and to provide care for the sufferers of the latter, respectively. Every year since then, the town of Santiago and the cathedral chapter have ceremoniously renewed their vow to the saint at the chapel, expressing their gratitude for his heavenly protection. As far as the hospital is concerned, it would appear that soon after it had come into operation —thanks largely to he support of Archbishop Francisco Blanco—, it became a centre dedicated to the treatment of venereal diseases, a function it served right up until the middle of this century. The hospital façade features the coat of arms of its founder and the statues of Cosme and Damian, the healing saints.

BANCO GALLEGO
TELEBANCO
CAJERO AUTOMATICO

Plaza de Cervantes, the square flanked in former times by shops selling country produce. In the background, the Church of San Benito.

Skirting the Hospital of San Roque on its right is Calle de las Ruedas, a street that takes us down to the place known as **Puerta del Camino,** so-called because it is the site of the town wall gate through which the most important section of the Camino or Pilgrim's Route once passed, the section that has since come to be known as the Castilian or French Route. Spreading out to our left as we stand at Puerta del Camino is a group of monumental buildings. First of all, there is the *Galician Centre for Contemporary Art,* recently built by Portuguese architect Alvaro Siza. Secondly, we have the *Monastery of Santo Domingo de Bonaval* (whose main building and church both belong to the 18th-century Baroque, even though the former preserves an east end from a 14th-century Gothic church). Nowadays the monastery houses the *Municipal Museum* (exhibiting, amongst other things, objects from the no-longer existing Hospital de los Reyes Católicos, for instance a portrait of Charles IV by Goya), the Museum of the Galician People (an ethnographical institution with rooms devoted to activities related to the sea and other traditional trades) and, in one of the church chapels, the *Pantheon of Illustrious Galicians* (holding the tombs of Rosalía de Castro, Ramón Cavanillas, Domingo Fontán, Alfredo Brañas, Castelao). Finally, there is a large park which, likewise remodelled by the architect Siza, combines the former orchard belonging to the monastery of Santo Domingo with what had been the local cemetery from 1947 until the middle of this century.

Galician Centre for Contemporary Art, the work of Portuguese architect Álvaro Siza.

Monastery of Santo Domingo de Bonaval.

Museo do Pobo Galego (Museum of the Galician People). Room dedicated to traditional seafaring activities.

We leave the above area by taking *Calle de Ramón del Valle Inclán,* which leads us back to *Calle de San Roque.* On this occasion we turn right into this road and follow it down to the end, where we find, facing each other on opposite sides of the street, the *Convent of Santa Clara* and that of *El Carmen.* The first of these convents, lying on our right, is run by nuns of the Order of St Clare and is believed to have been founded in the 13th century by queen Violante, the wife of Alfonso X the Wise; its present-day building, however, is 18th-century Baroque. The second belongs to a community of Discalced Carmelite nuns and was itself established in 1753 by the venerable Mother María Antonia de Jesús. Setting off down *Avenida de Coimbra,* the avenue that starts right in front of the Convent of Santa Clara, we join *Avenida de Juan XXIII,* which is lined on either side —behind large garden areas— by buildings belonging to the University, the area as a whole being referred to as the northern campus (including the Faculties of Economics and Business Studies and Modern Languages, along with the School of Nursing and the Primary School Teachers' Training College). The said landscaped area, which goes under the name of Parque de Vite or Parque del Burgo de las Naciones, is commanded by a building of large dimensions partially encircled by a small artificial lake. This is the *Auditorium of Galicia,* an excellent venue for concerts and exhibitions built by Spanish architect Julio Cano Laso, who died recently.

Convent of Santa Clara.